Laura and Almanzo at
Rocky Ridge Farm c.1913

William Anderson

2014

Laura Wilder
of Mansfield

by
William Anderson

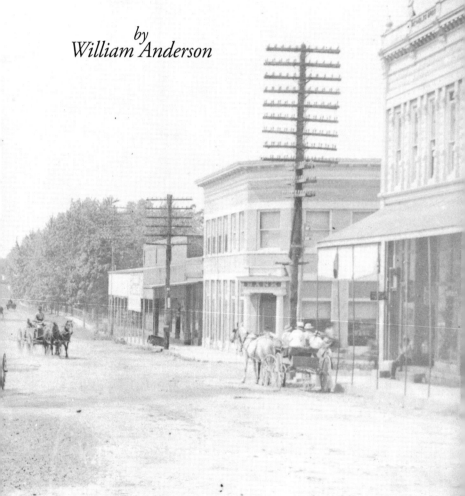

Foreword

What is it about favorite authors that make their writings inspire us enough to take up residence in our own lives and spirits? We re-read, re-think, and gain perennial wisdom from their published words. We continue to seek more understanding of their lives and times. Research is ongoing, and the unanswerable questions inspire debate and curiosity. Perhaps best of all, we are able to visit the homes, haunts, and writing locales of our favorite writers. Those before us assured that today's seekers can find tangible mementoes of the great ones' lives.

Laura Ingalls Wilder is an American classic author who inspires such allegiance. Millions of students sat spellbound in classrooms, reliving frontier life through Wilder's books, as patient teachers exposed us to the *Little House* books. I was one of those elementary students. For me, hearing about pioneer life inspired me to become a reader, become fascinated with history, and finally become an educator and a researcher and a writer myself. And along the way, I was able to lend a hand in the preservation of the Ingalls-Wilder family history.

The original *Laura Wilder of Mansfield* was the first attempt at a biography of Laura Ingalls Wilder. It was written for the Laura Ingalls Wilder Home & Museum in Mansfield, Missouri. Rose Wilder Lane wrote me, "I wish you every good fortune with it..." and she placed a copy in her Vermont library. Several editions of *Laura Wilder of Mansfield* have appeared, along with many other books about this family. This is the final edition! In it, I have tried to focus on Almanzo and Laura Wilder's lives in the community where they lived most of their lives. Their impact was strong, aside from the fact that Laura and her daughter Rose brought literary fame to the town.

The Wilders left behind extraordinary traces of their personal and professional lives. I hope some of the details included herein will give you another glimpse into their long, productive years in Mansfield.

WTA
April 2012

Cooley photo courtesy of N.L. Cleaveland; others from the Herbert Hoover Presidential Library, public domain publications and private collections.

Opening page sketch by Missouri author/illustrator *Cheryl Harness*

A special thanks to *Ann Weller Dahl* for expert editorial advice

Book Design: *Dixon Graphics,* Lapeer,MI

Early day Mansfield as the Wilders knew it. Cumberland Presbyterian Church is a prominent landmark in the background.

I. "This Is Where We Stop"

As the wagon rounded a curve and the town of Mansfield, Missouri appeared, 27 year old Laura Wilder said hopefully, "This is where we stop." With her husband, Almanzo, (called Manly), and their seven year daughter Rose, Laura was ready to end a long journey from drought-stricken South Dakota. It was the end of August 1894, and behind them was a rigorous trip with dust, heat and rough roads.

With the Wilders were Frank and Emma Cooley and their boys, Paul and George. They too were refugees from DeSmet, South Dakota. Though Laura described their trip as "one long picnic" for the three children, the adults were soberly apprehensive. Would Missouri provide the new life they sought?

The Cooleys: Emma, Paul, Frank, and George before leaving DeSmet, on the trek to Missouri with the Wilders.

Both families were enticed to Missouri's Ozarks by real estate and railroad advertisements. Promoters were hard pressed to sell the rocky, marginal land of the region. The soil would not sustain large scale agriculture, but smaller plots for "independent-minded farmers" sustained fruit, poultry, and cattle. Around Mansfield, "apples, peaches, strawberries and pears are practically sure crops." The area was called "The Land of the Big Red Apple."

Railroads were anxious to move people to the region, but the Wilders and Cooleys made the 45 day trip with teams and wagons. Frank Cooley took over management of the hotel and lunch room in the town of 800 people. The Wilders sought out a farm.

During their nine year marriage, Laura and Manly had experienced failure of their homestead, loss of a son, destruction of their home by fire, and financial ruin. Even worse was Manly's bout with "paralysis", most likely polio. The small but vigorous man was left with a limp and limited strength. The promise of a milder climate and small scale farming lured them to Missouri, far more than large red apples on glossy advertisements.

Manly's life was rooted in farming. He was born in 1857 on his family's farm in Malone, New York. He went west with his parents to another farm in Spring Valley, Minnesota, and was raising wheat on his own at 20. He loved horses, the land, and independence. In 1879 he filed on homestead land near DeSmet, Dakota Territory. There he met and married Laura Ingalls in 1885.

Laura's was a frontier childhood. Her first memories were of her 1867 birthplace in the woods of Wisconsin, followed by ten years of seeking a home in the west. Her family pioneered in Kansas, Minnesota, Iowa, and Dakota Territory. In 1879 the Ingalls family settled not far from Manly on the Dakota plains. There Laura attended school, taught school, and married Manly when she was 18. Their daughter Rose was born in 1886, followed by an infant son

A very early photo of Rocky Ridge Farm, with Manly and team.

who lived only a few short weeks. Though they loved the prairies, the Wilders were defeated by repeated dry years, crop losses and debt.

Missouri's Ozarks were lush, green, and fruitful, not unlike Laura's Wisconsin origins. It was a land of steep ridges, valleys, tumbling springs, shady oak woods, and rock formations. Because the hills were really valleys, the skyline was level. Laura hoped what she read about Mansfield was true …"that all seeking homes in the healthy and productive locality may be assured of a welcome and fair treatment by hospitable inhabitants."

A mile from Mansfield's town square was a crazy quilt-patch of rough land covered with rocks, old oaks, brush, and knobby hills. A deep ravine gashed the land and a spring bubbled up at its bottom. When rains fell, a creek trickled around the base of the hill where a road led to a log cabin. Laura was enchanted with the place but Manly was dubious. He was accustomed to flat, tillable prairie. But Laura prevailed. "The forty" was bought for $10 an acre from The Bank of Mansfield. On September 21, 1894, the Wilders paid $100 as a down payment, assuming a tree lien. The previous owner left hundreds of burlap-wrapped apple seedlings, and so the Wilders were automatically fruit farmers.

Laura, Manly and Rose settled into the cabin at the edge of the ravine. Laura named their land Rocky Ridge Farm. Though picturesque, the place needed nurture before it would reap even a grudging return. During the first winter the raspy crosscut saw sounded over the land as Manly and Laura cleared trees away to create space for the orchard. Manly peddled stove wood in town, providing a scant income. This pattern of subsidizing the farm with outside income persisted for years to come.

While her parents worked, Rose explored the farm. She was a shy, quiet child, with an active internal life enriched by books and stories. Undemonstrative, she "understood" her parents' struggles. In the spring of 1895 she helped plant the first corn crop, and she picked wild berries to sell in town. She walked a mile over the hills to attend Mansfield school, later riding a donkey. Her playmates were the Cooley boys; her inclusion in school life was a slow process.

Within two years Manly built a frame addition to the cabin, and then switched the building site altogether. On log skids the frame structure was re-located nearby. This small house with sleeping loft for Rose was the first triumph on Rocky Ridge. The old cabin became the barn, which expanded through the years. The Wilders felt rich when they could afford a cow and a pig, and in 1897 they bought six more acres of land. Progress was slow and steady on Rocky Ridge but the farm did not turn enough profit to support a family of three.

II. The Mansfield Years 1898-1910

Frank Cooley's sudden death in 1898 opened a way for Manly to earn regular wages. Cooley was Mansfield's drayman, and Manly bought his team and wagon and continued the delivery and hauling service. The Wilders moved to town and rented a yellow frame house. They still worked the farm, but were now town folks. Manly became an agent for Waters Pierce Oil Company, delivering kerosene, oil and other products. Laura handled the accounting.

In 1898 Manly's parents and his older sister Laura visited Mansfield en route to Louisiana where they planned to settle. During their stay Grandpa Wilder purchased the rented town house and presented the deed to Manly and Laura. The older Wilders grieved over Manly's disability and the hard times he had endured, and their gift was a significant one; the Wilders inched into the middle class of Mansfield.

They also made inroads into community life. Old timers remembered Manly driving a perfectly matched team hitched to a light wagon in an early July 4th parade. Behind her parents, standing in the wagon, Rose represented Liberty. She made a pleasing picture, with her unbraided long hair flowing loose, wearing a patriotic sash across her white dress. These holiday celebrations gave Mansfield people a chance to show their community pride, mingle, picnic, and listen to local talent present music and speeches.

The Mansfield Square was the chief gathering spot for towns-people, and the Wilders joined their friends and neighbors there for concerts, socials, and patriotic events.

Mansfield Methodist Church

Mansfield businesses were built around the Town Square.
The livery stable was a familiar place for Manly.

The Wilders attended the Methodist Episcopal congregation even before the church had a building. The Methodists used the Cumberland Presbyterian sanctuary until their own church was built. The frame church building was constructed on the Hartville Road, just north of the town square, with dedication services at Christmas 1899. Laura organized the church's first bazaar; she was among the core of hard working church ladies from the start. Laura's gingerbread became locally famous, and this became her staple contribution for church dinners, socials and club meetings.

At the turn of the twentieth century small towns across America offered a variety of social and fraternal organizations, with deep bonds of friendship developing among the membership. Mansfield had its Eden Club, an Odd Fellows lodge, Modern Woodmen lodge, and the Masonic Order. Manly and Laura had ties with the latter, having been members in DeSmet. So Manly attended Masonic meetings on Wednesdays, "on or before the full moon." When the Mansfield chapter of Order of the Eastern Star formed in 1897, Laura was a member. In 1902 Manly also joined. He made and contributed flower stands, emblems, and staffs for the chapter. Together, he and Laura brought in 20 new members.

Laura was active in Eastern Star for forty years. She filled many roles: conductress, secretary, and district deputy grand lecturer. She served as Worthy Matron twice. After her second tenure as Worthy Matron, Laura received a gift, and the minutes recorded that "Sister

Wilder being completely taken by surprise was unable to fitly express her thanks…" Laura was often asked to install officers because of her eloquence and ability to memorize the rituals. The group enjoyed a variety of activities: quilting, New Year's Watch Parties, play performances, and good plain fellowship. "Peace and harmony prevailing" was the way Laura summarized the meetings while recording the minutes as secretary.

Town life gave Rose the chance to join her classmates' social activities. She was a talented, but often a bored student; today she would be called "gifted." Rose was alternately frustrated, willful, and as she said, "mad at the teacher." What her parents thought of this is unrecorded, but they did not insist that she attend school. Instead Rose spent many days in the hayloft of the barn reading insatiably. She borrowed all the books she could find, and her education was self-directed. She dreamily wrote stories, sketched, designed monograms, and published her first writing in the school news section of the *Mansfield Mail*.

Rose as a career girl.

Rose took friends to Rocky Ridge to picnic and play in the ravine. The girls snitched apples from the orchards (the Wilder orchard didn't start bearing until circa 1902). When the circus came to town, Rose considered running away with the show. Leaving home became a reality in 1903 when Manly's sister Eliza Jane invited Rose to spend a school year with her in Crowley, Louisiana. The high school there offered Latin, which Rose longed to study. The year in Crowley was Rose's first adventure away from her Papa and Mama Bess, the nickname she used for Laura. To Manly and to close friends Laura was "Bessie."

The Wilders continued to live frugally. They sold a little farm produce, but absentee farming was never very profitable. Laura sold her excess butter for ten cents a pound. With the extra funds, the Wilders purchased additional acres to enlarge Rocky Ridge. They added an additional forty acres in 1899. In 1905 they bought another twelve acres. The process continued; at its largest the farm was somewhere between 185 and 200 acres "more or less", as deeds read.

Laura was ambitious to succeed financially and socially. The Wilders regarded marriage as a partnership, and Laura was eager to

Laura (circled) and three other women officially "drove the golden spike" to mark the construction start of the 16 mile railroad live from Mansfield to Ava. The electric line encouraged trade and pleasure trips between the towns.

participate economically. She did what she could: opened her home to boarders. N.J. Craig, cashier at The Bank of Mansfield, lived with the Wilders. "Jeff" became their close friend, and when he founded the competing Farmers and Merchants Bank in 1908, they supported it. Another roomer and boarder was John Quigley.

In 1908 when the Bluebird Railroad was under construction, Laura cooked for the railway officials. When she set her table for paying boarders, she did it cheerfully. She cooked economically, but created tasty meals. A friend noted that "Mrs. Wilder could get more for her money than anyone."

There was room in the little house in Mansfield for boarders, for Rose had left home. After her year in Crowley Rose learned telegraphy in the Mansfield depot. She took a job as an operator in Kansas City, joining the ranks of "bachelor girls" entering the job market in the early twentieth century. Laura combined an Eastern Star meeting with a visit to Rose in the fall of 1906, traveling by train.

Laura started a pattern of trip-taking without Manly when she traveled to South Dakota at the time of her father's death in 1902. She continued her jaunts for Eastern Star events. When she grew active in the Democratic Party, she went to various meetings around Missouri. In 1908 she traveled to Sedalia to visit Mrs. Quigley, and though Manly was willing to let her go, the *Mansfield Press* hinted that he was lonely without her. *"Mr. Wilder,"* the paper said, *"was anxiously looking for his wife last Saturday, but don't want to let on, though, and don't want us to say anything about it."*

This was unusual, a wife traveling without her husband, but the Wilders had the cachet of being slightly unconventional, further enhanced by Rose's career in the big city. By 1907, she left Kansas City to become manager of the Western Union office in Mount Vernon, Indiana. In 1908 she was a telegrapher at the Fairmont Hotel in San Franciso, and Gillette Lane was courting her. They were married in March 1909, and Rose remained a working woman, again an unusual deviation from customs of the era.

Manly's endless routes through the countryside as a drayman and deliveryman were diminishing. Automobiles were visible in the Ozarks now, despite the primitive roads. When the Bluebird Railroad linked Mansfield to Ava, the needs for Manly's services were reduced. He and Laura decided to resume fulltime farming. They sold the Mansfield house to Mr. Craig early in 1910, and in the spring they moved back to their farm.

Laura and Manly were returning to their original goal, Rocky Ridge Farm.

III. Back to the Farm

Rocky Ridge consisted of 100 acres of improved land when the Wilders returned. The tamed land contained a thriving orchard, smooth green slopes for cattle grazing, and cleared fields for crops. The summer of 1910 was the start of a new era for the farm; the expectation was that the land alone would essentially support the family.

Rose spent several months at home that summer. She and Gillette re-settled in Kansas City, partially to be closer to Laura and Manly. But Rose's writing job on the *Kansas City Post* was on hold because of a difficult pregnancy, the child's death in May, and a harrowing surgery. While Gillette traveled, pursuing business ventures, Rose recuperated on the farm.

Laura in the ravine, 1910

Summer was the farm's busiest season, but Laura and Rose relaxed in the ravine, took tea in a tent pitched near the house, and doted on Robin Hood, the pet colt. It was an optimistic time, for the farm, for Rose's career and marriage, and for Laura's plan to write for publication. Rose prodded Mama Bess, helping with her poetry, and writing voice. Laura was already known as an advocate for farm families, and an interview with her appeared in *The American Food Journal* in September 1910.

Through that summer of '10, Manly's helper on the farm was young Julian Bucher, from Kansas City. Julian adored the Wilders; to them he seemed a son and brother. A progression of hired men worked with Manly, but none enjoyed the family feeling Julian felt. When work was done he joined the Wilders for picnics, hikes, and buggy rides. And how he enjoyed Laura's tasty meals!

The Wilders slipped into the cycle of seasons that framed a farm. Manly planted potatoes "by the dark of the moon". Strawberries were the first spring crop. New refrigerated railroad cars whisked fruit to St. Louis and Kansas City within a day of picking. Garden stuff supplied Laura's table all summer, while field crops ripened. She canned excess for winter use, storing the crocks in the neat cellar that Manly created. Manly hayed as many times as he could, depending on the rainfalls and weather, stuffing the barn for the next winter.

One liners and brief bits in *The Mansfield Mirror* shed light on what was raised on Rocky Ridge. Timothy and sheaf Sudan grass were mentioned, and millet (oats). Corn cutting was reported in September. Manly brought in record-sized rhubarb stalks to show the editor

Laura and Rose at apple picking time.

and reported that his strawberries evaded spring frost. He used the newspaper to warn off hunters from his farm, especially after his horse and a sow were accidentally shot. Quail hunting was also forbidden, as the birds kept the orchard safe from insects.

The thin layer of top soil on the farm required nurture, with tons of added lime, and fertilizer. Crop rotation was practiced. Nearby neighboring farms were "corned to death", with no thought of conservation of the soil. The Wilders studied regular farm bulletins to learn of current practices. They were early conservationists and stewards of the land.

By 1910, the apple trees planted in 1895 became the lush Wilder orchard. There were also peaches and pears. When the trees were heavy with ripened fruit, they were picked and packed in barrels. One tree yielded five barrels of #1 grade apples. Shipped out by railroad carloads to big cities, the orchard was a key cash crop.

Other cash income came from the herd of Jersey cows. Cream checks brought in weekly income. Contented cows grazed on the green grassy spaces on Rocky Ridge. Laura tended the chickens and turkeys. Logging expenses, the Wilders discovered that cream and eggs each netted equal profits. Laura studied poultry-raising data, and became an expert on the topic.

In 1911, when the Wright County Agricultural Fair and Stock Show, "The World's fair of the Ozarks" debuted in Mansfield, Rocky

Ridge products won premiums. Manly pitched in to judge the Horse and Mule Division, and he and Laura alternated as poultry judges.

The success of the Wilder farm was noticed throughout Wright County and beyond. A newspaper editorialized: *"Mr. Wilder is a model farmer…(he) shows a greater percent of actual profit than anyone we know… An hour spent at Rocky Ridge Farm would, in our opinion, be more beneficial than to spend a week at any state poultry farm …"*

The local fame of Rocky Ridge linked Laura to writing jobs in regional farm papers. Her first submissions, mostly on poultry, were for *The Star Farmer*, published in St. Louis. This was a low rung of journalism, but as Rose later said, Hemingway got his start on *The Kansas City Post*. Laura was back on the farm less than a year when she advanced to the *Missouri Ruralist*, a larger farm weekly. Her feature story "Favors the Farm Home" was published in the *Ruralist* in February 1911. It was followed by "The Story of Rocky Ridge Farm" in July. Both articles extolled the potentials of farm life.

Manly & Julian Bucher in the oat field.

"I am in on the ground floor!" Laura reported happily of her new career. But the farm work came first, although it was a springboard for most of Laura's writing topics in her earliest publications. "Bully for you, Mama Bess!", Rose exclaimed, when she read Laura's work. She was always supportive and a savvy advisor.

Laura and Manly worked as a congenial team in the farm business. Although Laura agreed with women's suffrage, she never identified with the women's movement itself. She was comfortable as her husband's equal. They consulted on all business decisions. When needed, she helped Manly with physical labor; he was never again the robust man he had been in his youth.

Laura's role as farm wife was arduous. Housekeeping was primitive, especially on an isolated farm. She tended her hens, cooked meals that included hired help at the table, tended garden, baked bread, churned, laboriously laundered, canned, and cleaned. Sometimes stress drove her to the woods, where the world of nature gave respite.

Rocky Ridge never made much money, but it was the Wilders' chosen life. Rose fussed over her parents' hard work, and helped financially when she could. This became a focal point of her life, constant dedication to easing her parents' lives. She and Gillette re-settled in northern California, selling real estate in the pre-World War I land boom. Rose was a career woman; she had no hope of motherhood.

After two years back on the farm, the Wilders decided to complete the house begun in the '90s. Yes, the farm looked promising enough to expand the cramped original home. In September, 1913, the local newspaper reported that *"A.J. Wilder is building a fine ... residence ..."*

Manly ceded most of the planning to Laura. Her notion was the romantic idea that a house must harmonize with the land. Her vision was a rustic frame house, with sweeping lines, and native rock chimney.

An early sketch of the completed house.
Gray trim contrasted with the overall white paint.

The building site was at the edge of the ravine, atop a tree covered hill. Field stones formed the foundation, and cured oak made a stout frame. Windows were everywhere, linking the interior to the outdoors. Thrift was important, but not at the cost of beauty. The pine lumber for lap siding and the labor were the biggest expenses.

While Manly had ability as a carpenter, the addition to the house was major construction, so Ezra Dennis, a fine local builder, was hired for the job. By the end of 1913 the project was mostly complete. The house was an organic process; through upcoming decades, it was a work-in-progress. When finished, the house had three porches, and huge windows, looking out on the rolling land. Laura may have been influenced by Frank Lloyd Wright's "organic harmony" style. The interior of the house certainly reflects Wright's "open plan", with living room, dining room and library flowing together.

Clippings and photos saved by Laura indicate that she was looking for inspiration. The parlor's beams, boxy support posts, open stairway, and oak paneling gave the interior a woodsy look. The rough hewn fireplace, formed from three immense rocks, was Laura's heartfelt request, though the builders balked at handling the girth of the stones.

The upstairs had a guest bedroom, a wide hallway room, and a sleeping porch.

It was an abrupt visual change, crossing the threshold from the original downstairs rooms (now the woodshed-entry, kitchen, and bedroom) to the "new" part of the house. The atmosphere was far sturdier and grander than the original construction. Off the bedroom was a primitive water closet (later, Laura's office), the dining room (eventually the "music room"), and the spacious parlor-library. *Missouri Opportunities* said it best: *"A beautiful modern home crowns the farm of the Wilders."*

The Wilder house became a social center. Easter Sunday sunrise services were held on the grassy slope. An engagement party was hosted. Laura's friends arrived to socialize. Meetings and dances happened in the parlor. Company came for meals. Laura planned a candle-lit theme party, with guests wearing vintage clothing. Old time games were played in the flickering candle flames. The local newspaper called it *"one of the delightful events of the season."*

The Wilders surprised a 1917 Eastern Star meeting held at the Mansfield lodge hall, asking chapter members to adjourn to the farm. A social columnist outdid him (or her?) self, with compliments.

"Three cars conveyed the merry crowd to Rocky Ridge Farm, where the oak paneled, oak beamed living room was alight from the fire in the large fireplace and the glow of rose-shaded lamps from the dining room. Delicious and unique refreshments were served during the evening. The table decorations were in the Star colors, the centerpiece being the regular Star emblem…The edibles…were also in the proper colors. After lunch the guests gathered in the firelight and listened to the wonderful violin music of Kreisler and Erman, selections from well-known operas, Victor Herbert's orchestra and Hawaiian stringed instruments. The music was furnished by a Victrola, the Christmas gift of Rose Wilder Lane of San Francisco…with music and conversation, the time passed without a dull moment and the guests departed, regretting that the evening had been too short."

"Make your little farm home noted for its hospitality," Laura wrote in *The Missouri Ruralist*. Bound up in the boards and beams of their home was the contentment of a couple, who worked and planned together.

IV. "I Have Always Been A Busy Person"
— Laura Ingalls Wilder

Carrie Ingalls told Laura, "You are so busy doing, you never stop to see what you have done." Carrie made two visits to the Wilders before her 1912 marriage, and she saw her energetic sister combine farm work, church, organizations, and a career as a country journalist. Indeed, the decade of 1910-1920 was perhaps a time of greatest activity for both Wilders.

Laura was forced to take respite when hospitalized for surgery in the fall of 1912. By November she was home, and eleven friends dropped in to visit, and admired the way Manly kept his cellar. From DeSmet, Laura's mother wrote, advising her to sleep soundly and not work so hard.

That was difficult advice for Laura to follow. She became a semi-regular contributor to the *Missouri Ruralist*. After years of writing poetry, and hoping to join Rose in the writing field, it happened. The *Ruralist* editor, John Case, encouraged submissions from "Mrs. A.J. Wilder", as her by-line read. From 1911 to 1915 she published a handful of pieces, all farm topics. Those dealing with the Wilders' own experience on Rocky Ridge are a goldmine of data on the farm's development.

Laura's photo appeared in the Ruralist, along with articles by and about her.

Rose was full of advice for her mother; buy a typewriter, she urged. Laura did. Re-sell any articles she could, slightly revised, she said. Use speeches she made at meetings as copy to sell.

Rose deplored her parents' hard work, and that "everything goes back into the farm." Pushing thirty, she worked long hours as well, writing for *The San Francisco Bulletin*. She started there as an editorial assistant, moving on to write feature stories, serial fiction, and interviews with greats … like Charlie Chaplin, Henry Ford, and aviator Art Smith.

After their mutual run in California real estate flopped, Rose and Gillette settled on Russian Hill. Gillette's career floundered, while Rose became visible as a San Francisco journalist. The marriage was strained; a family friend simply said, "Rose was carrying them both." They were in debt to Mama Bess and Manly, and Rose drove herself to afford life in a big city. When the 1915 San Francisco World's Fair opened, Rose begged her parents to visit.

There was a compromise: Laura made the trip, spending two months with Rose. She disliked leaving Manly and the hired man alone to handle fall farm work, but Rose supplied money to compensate for Laura's absence. The trip was a whirlwind of experiences for Laura: the Fair, the beauty of the Bay region, reunion with Rose, city life, and observing her daughter's career. Rose mentored her Mama Bess's writing as never before.

An order came from *Missouri Ruralist* for Laura to cover the Fair, especially the Missouri building at the exposition. This December, 1915 piece "And Missouri 'Showed' Them" was a breakthrough. In 1916 and 1917 she appeared in the farm weekly more frequently.

Mrs. A. J. Wilder developed a reputation as a farm expert; she participated in and founded organizations for rural families in the region. Tips on poultry raising, farm life, interviews, and cheery essays on life gave her an audience. John Case gave her two regular columns: *"As a Farm Women Thinks"* and *"The Farm Home"*. Her essays, sometimes prosy, show Laura's ethics and beliefs. She was

"We do enjoy sitting around the fireplace in the evening and on stormy days."

democratic in her thinking, supporting fair treatment for all. She detested sexism, racism, and child labor.

Laura's writing enhanced her status as a lifelong learner. Evenings with Manly usually involved reading and discussing current events and farm issues. The well stocked parlor library included many classics, lighter adventure novels, humor, and eventually books authored by Rose. The pump organ stood in the "Music Room" next to the victrola. The records ranged from "Carmen" and "Nutcracker" by Victor Herbert's Orchestra to "After the Ball was Over" and "Rocky Mountain Moon." Recordings by stars of the era made the Wilders familiar with Geraldine Farrar, Fritz Kreisler, the Peerless Quartette, and Mischa Ellman.

Laura claimed she was not musical, except for "a little music in

*"We're going to be late getting the hay in...can't you come and rake it for us",
said Manly. Laura later said, "I could and I DID; also I drove the team on the
hay fork to fill the big barn, for such is the life of a farmer's wife ..."*

her feet". Laura and Manly went dancing with Jeff and Ella Craig.
Manly was mostly sidelined by his lame foot. Mr. Craig not only
owned the Farmers and Merchants Bank, but was also a prominent
attorney, often in Hartville, the county seat. In 1916 Laura and
Ella were invited to join the elite Athenian Club in Hartville. It was
a study club, with protocol and goals. This fit well with Laura's
reputation as an intellectual.

Current events, book reviews, musical and dramatic performances
by members filled Athenian sessions, followed by social hours. One
year was devoted to study authors: Mark Twain, Shakespeare,
Dickens, Hawthorne, Holmes, and Scott among them. Laura
reported on *The Old Curiosity Shop, As You Like It,* and *Joan of Arc.*
Manly drove Laura and Ella to Hartville, a twelve mile trip, and
killed time at the court house checker games until the meetings were
over. When the Craigs acquired a car and the road improved, the
trip was easier. The Athenian club members anticipated the yearly
meeting held at the beautiful Wilder place.

While Laura pursued her interests, Manly varied the farm's crops
and techniques. He crafted unique furniture and cabinetry for the
farmhouse. There were five springs on the farm, and Manly harnessed
one 1400 feet above the house and barn to provide running water.

Manly and "The Governor"

The water ran downhill through pipes two feet underground. Hydrants provided water to the henhouse, the barn, the orchard, the garden, and the house. No more hauling water from the ravine spring. Manly ran a pipe through the kitchen cook stove ... hot *and* cold running water poured through the sink faucets.

Manly was well known in town and country as a keen wit, a storyteller, an expert farmer and a horseman. He always favored the Morgan horse for its strength, appearance, good nature and flexibility.

From the American Remount Association, Manly leased the "Governor of Orleans", a bay stallion. Manly wished to upgrade local horseflesh and Governor sired many colts. The Wilders loved Governor; Manly said Morgans had more intelligence than any breed of horse.

In 1917, the Wilders supported the formation of the Mansfield Farm Loan Association. This was a local branch of the Federal Land Bank, started by Act of Congress in 1916. Long term loans were offered to farmers at far lower interest rates than banks allowed. Laura became Secretary-Treasurer. She handled paperwork and completed loan applications, receiving a modest income. She did business in an office room on Mansfield's square. Her work was praised by national examiners, and while she served there were no defaults or payment delays. During her tenure, well into the 1920s, she handled a million dollars in government loans. She electrified those around her when a man of color came into her office for loan applications and she readily shook his hand.

When America entered World War I in 1918, a huge demand for farm products resulted. Rocky Ridge did its part. Laura's *Ruralist* articles focused on patriotism, sacrifice, and the role of the home front. The Wilders served on the Red Cross Auction project, donating farm products for the cause. Laura worked with the Red Cross making night shirts and surgical bandages for the boys in military hospitals. When the war ended, she helped with a homecoming for the returning soldiers.

In 1919, when women could vote, Laura wrote that "It will be interesting to observe how they will respond to the duty." She promptly became chairman of the county Democratic committee, and traveled to Rolla for state meetings.

As she entered her fifties, Laura juggled homemaking, farming, writing, community and church work, a Farm Loan job, and busy social life. Her sister Grace asked her: "Why do you work so hard, Laura?"

V. The 1920s: Times of Change

While the Wilders lived on the farm, and were well known among Mansfield's residents, Rose thrived in the big city. Her first novel appeared as *Diverging Roads,* a small-town-girl's career and romance in California, not unlike Rose's history. The heroine is bedazzled by a confident but superficial man, not unlike Gillette. They marry, but grow apart and divorce.

In 1918, after long intervals of living apart, Rose and Gillette Lane divorced. No doubt Rose's parents disliked the divorce, and small town Mansfield commented on it. But they understood that Rose was better off without the feckless Gillette Lane. He remarried two more times.

While Laura's writing progressed, Rose's was on a grander scale. She was sent to Hollywood to cover the silent film industry . . . interviewing the great stars of the time. Her walking tour through northern California became the serial "Soldiers of the Soil", focusing on the wartime demand for food. A farm girl herself, this suited her well. Rose's "The City at Night" was an expose of San Francisco after dark. "The Building of Hetch Hetchy" informed readers of the massive project to provide San Francisco with a reliable water supply. Rose later commented that her best writing could be found in the morgue of *The San Francisco Bulletin.*

Not as successful were her "fictionalized biographies" of Henry Ford, Herbert Hoover, Jack London, and Charlie Chaplin. London's widow disliked Rose's invention of dialogue and romanticizing. Chaplin ordered Rose's story of his life suppressed in book form. None of the men expressed pleasure with Rose's technique.

Rose lived in a place she called "Little House on Telegraph Hill." There she found the life she wanted, as an independent career woman. She entertained often, and mingled with intellectuals, fellow writers, and artists. Her roommate was illustrator Berta Hoerner, who remained a good friend after her wedding to artist Elmer Hader.

In 1918 Rose resigned from the *Bulletin*, beginning again as a freelance writer. The Red Cross hired her to write about its efforts, and Rose worked for a month in Washington, during which time The Great War ended. She then moved to Greenwich Village, again sharing quarters with Berta. An article for *Ladies' Home Journal* brought Rose $750, a huge coup. Mama Bess was interested in such things.

Rose's publishing connections brought her mother's name to its first national exposure in June 1919, with an article in *McCall's.* The magazine ran a series on occupations of men, and how wives were helpmeets. With Rose's help, Laura wrote about a farmer's wife, posing as advisor to a young woman who inquires about life on a farm. Rose edited the piece, making it publishable. The fee and her first byline as Laura Ingalls Wilder quelled Mama Bess's annoyance with Rose's heavy edit.

Laura and Manly's wandering daughter paid them a long visit that summer of 1919. Flush with cash from a ghost-writing job, Rose settled into the sleeping porch of the farmhouse, using it as both a bedroom and an office.

Mama Bess had just helped found The Justamere Club in town, dedicated to study and current events. When she hosted the August meeting, Rose was the star, giving "a most interesting talk concerning instances connected with her stay in New York." Though Rose was welcomed, some townspeople whispered about the source of her income and activities in big cities. Mansfield never understood Rose.

Athenian Club members described her as "bohemian".

Rose received an invitation from the American Red Cross to go to Europe to report on its massive postwar work in ravaged countries. She also got magazine assignments for future stories from Europe. Rose sailed in May, 1920; three years elapsed until she returned home to Mansfield.

The Wilders received reams of typewritten letters from Rose … from London, Paris, Geneva, Vienna, Prague, Warsaw. Laura thriftily used them in her Ruralist columns. For the *Bulletin* Rose dispatched a travel series: "Come with Me to Europe." She went on to see Italy, Greece, Turkey, and Armenia, parts of Soviet Russia, Yugoslavia, Egypt, Iraq, and Albania. The Albanian mountains and people made a profound impression on Rose; she wrote of her adventures in the primitive country in *Peaks of Shala*.

While Rose traveled the world, her parents worked hard on Rocky Ridge Farm. The postwar slump reduced need for farm products; lower prices resulted. Laura quit the poultry business because higher expenses for feed cut her profits. Manly was past sixty and maneuvering the rocky hills was difficult for him.

In 1920, Rose offered her parents an annual $500, to free them from farm labor. She suggested a sale, ridding the place of unneeded

Laura and Manly in the 1920s at a friend's farm.

equipment, and selling land. Rose urged the folks to "think of Rocky Ridge as a country home, and not as a farm ..."

Laura and Manly appreciated Rose's support, continuing with smaller scale farming. Their products still won prizes at the county fair. Manly served on the Mansfield Fair committee's Horse and Mule division, and Laura was also involved.

At the end of 1923, Rose returned to Rocky Ridge, with trunk-fuls of gifts and curios, and amazing tales. She made the rounds of Mama Bess's clubs, but worked steadily on magazine submissions to replenish her funds. Helen Boylston, a war nurse, arrived to join the Wilders for long interludes; she and Rose met in Europe. Other writer friends arrived to visit. Manly made himself scarce during these onslaughts of vocal females. "A fellow can't even go to the *john* here," he grumbled, "there's always a hen on it." Yes, in 1924 the farmhouse was modernized with a bathroom in a former wood storage room. The kitchen, full of built-ins, was moved to a former entryway, and a porch was added. The dining room shifted into the

The new kitchen location with built-in storage areas.

former kitchen, and in its place was the Music Room, off the parlor. The farmhouse was a work-in-progress, with frequent innovations and updates. Rose ordered all new Simmons beds, and added fly-

Helen Boylston (Troub) at Rocky Ridge.

Helen later wrote career novels, including the "Sue Barton" nurse series.

❧

screens. At some point the water closet became Laura's writing study, with a new added window.

In 1925 Rose published *He Was a Man*, a book version of her Jack London series. *Hill Billy* was based on N.J. Craig; it was printed as a magazine serial and book. The Rose Wilder Lane byline appeared regularly in *The Country Gentleman* and other periodicals. Rose used proceeds to by a Buick sedan for her parents; their first car. Manly learned to drive well.

In 1925 Rose, Laura, and Helen (nicknamed Troub), made a road trip to California. The women visited Rose's San Francisco friends and old haunts. They drove down the Pacific coast, stopping in Los Angeles. They toured Universal Studios, but despite the exciting itinerary, Laura was homesick. She encouraged the quicker southern route for their return to Missouri.

Laura reached a turning point that year. She said she was "very near to nervous prostration." She confided to Manly that her work … at home, church, clubs, the farm loan business, and *Ruralist* writing … exhausted her. She often walked through her days in a haze. The state highway cut a swatch through Rocky Ridge, disturbing its peace and privacy, and the Wilders discussed selling out. They couldn't do it, realizing the place was made with their own hands and efforts.

Rose was anxious to travel again; she felt she had done her duty on the farm. In 1926 Rose and Troub went to Paris for language study. They bought a Model T Ford and drove to Albania, the land of Rose's obsession. The women settled in Tirana, and Rose resumed work at her typewriter; she could never neglect her writing career for long.

In those halcyon economic times of the late '20s, getting rich seemed a possibility. Rose and Troub, and later the Wilders, placed their savings with The Palmer Company, and watched the investments grow. There seemed no end to the boom, and Rose indulged in frantic consumerism. Her magazine prices soared, and she was considered one of the best paid writers in America.

Rose and Troub lived in Tirana until 1928. Rose drew a fanciful plan of a walled compound overlooking the Adriatic: her dream home. Then the era ended. Rose wrote and sold "Cindy" as a serial; she was paid $10,000. This Ozark story pained her, as she regarded it as trashy writing. But the money buoyed her on to her next plan, a return to the farm and building a new house for her parents.

Actually two new houses were constructed on the farm in 1928. The Wilders built a small rock sided cottage across the new highway, as a rental. It later it became a tenant house for Bruce Prock, who worked on the farm. Rose's project was an English-styled rock house, based on a Sears Roebuck plan. The site was ¾ mile through the woods from the farmhouse. Rose engaged an architect to customize the house.

Troub returned to live in the farmhouse with Rose, and the place was not large enough to house both generations, plus a parade of company. At one time four typewriters were clattering in the house, when writers visited. Rose's plan was to modernize the farmhouse for herself, and give her parents a completely modern, compact retirement home. Laura agreed, but refused to be involved with the plans or preparations. But Rose and Manly stood sentinel on the building site whenever work was done.

The house was started in August; five months later it was complete. The estimated cost was $5,500. After all of Rose's embellishments were added, the price doubled. Then she furnished the rooms lavishly. Her optimism matched the boom times. (Her magazine stories sold for $1,200 per; the average annual wage in 1928 was $1,296.) When finished, the new house was a showplace. When the furniture was in place, Laura and Manly moved in, at Christmas.

Rose wrote:"It's a darling cottage, sort of modified English ... done in field stone ... with brick window sills and a tiny bit of brick terrace. Only five rooms, but thoroughly well built ... Rol-Screens and brass pipes, hot and cold soft water ... electric range, electric refrigerator, tiled bathroom ... textured plaster for the walls. Steel door casings and steel casement windows and French doors ... I do hope the family will like it. My mother hasn't seen it yet; won't see it until it is all finished and furnished. She wanted a new house, but didn't want to bother with it in the building stages."

Laura had given up her Farm Loan job, and stopped her regular *Ruralist* writing; she and Manly appeared "retired". Manly was 71 and Laura 61 when the Rock House era started. Rose's royalties, and fees from *Harper's, Ladies Home Journal*, and *Pictorial Review*, kept cash flowing in. Rose coaxed Troub to write as well, so another author was at work in the farmhouse.

The Palmer Company paid dividends on the Wilder-Lane-Boylston accounts all through 1929. Then, less than a year after the Wilders settled into the Rock House, the stock market crashed.

VI. The 1930s: Writing Books

The onset of the Depression had little impact on Rocky Ridge. Rose's short stories sold, until magazines were cash-strapped. The Palmer Company paid dividends. Laura and Manly lived comfortably in the Rock House. Their car changed their lives. "They are going around and seeing the Ozarks, meeting new people, and having a happy time together," Rose said.

Manly mended fence, gardened, went to farm sales and auctions. He played pool in town. His lame foot was weaker; he cobbled his own shoes to accommodate his needs. He used a cane, but was a fit man for seventy-plus, other than a brief bout with lip cancer. Manly still hitched up old Buck to plow up patches of land. Jack, the burro, pulled loads of wood. Manly brought a small herd of Saannen milk goats to the farm. Laura was not pleased over the goats, though she got used to using the milk, making butter and cheese.

Laura discovered that a modern house made light work. She entertained for dinner, for bridge, and club meetings. She and Rose visited often, wearing a path between the two houses. Troub joined them for shopping trips to Springfield and St. Louis. They saw movies like "Rin-Tin-Tin." Laura favored adventure stories, and during 1929, she decided that her own life was worth telling.

In school tablets, Laura wrote of her growing up years. She told of the covered wagon moves, log cabins and claim shanties, hardships and happiness. The manuscript was called "Pioneer Girl." Rose took it, typed it and edited it. Rose's agent tried selling the memoir but it was not grist for commercial publication. Instead, it was the first step in the writing the *Little House* books.

Rose's friends, Berta and Elmer Hader were an illustrating team, publishing children's picture books. When Laura re-worked "Pioneer Girl" into a children's book, the Haders used connections, and *Little House in the Big Woods* was sold to Harper & Brothers in 1931.

While the book was in the making, Laura and Manly returned to their prairie past. They drove to South Dakota. In DeSmet, little seemed familiar. They discovered they were seeking their lost youth. Laura's sister Grace and her husband welcomed them. They crossed South Dakota, arriving in the Black Hills, where Carrie lived at Keystone. Near her house was Mount Rushmore, where Washington's head was already carved on the mountain. After seeing the Black Hills, Laura and Manly headed home.

*Rose Wilder Lane
at Rocky Ridge …
in a publicity photo
promoting her novel
"Old Home Town",
published by
Longmans, Green & Co.
on October 5, 1935.
"Little House on the Prairie"
was published a few
days earlier.*

That fall, the Depression hit Rocky Ridge. The Palmer Company collapsed, wiping out Rose, her parents, and Troub. Troub hastily got a nursing job, and headed east. Rose was left responsible for the farm. She carefully hid her stress and frustration with life on Rocky Ridge.

In April 1932 *Little House in the Big Woods* was published. A small edition was printed, with illustrations by Helen Sewell. The first small royalties were, Laura said, "a regular budget of good cheer." "I just started writing one book," Laura said, but she followed it with *Farmer Boy*. It was about Manly's boyhood on a New York farm. The book required a rewrite, but Harper published it in 1933.

At the same time Rose used family lore for a serial: "Let the Hurricane Roar." The story of hard times and homesteading appeared in *The Saturday Evening Post*. It resonated with Americans coping with the Depression's challenges. The book version was popular when it debuted in 1933, but Mama Bess was displeased.

Laura felt Rose pirated her material in *Let the Hurricane Roar*. Rose believed the audience was different than her mother's children's book … and that *Hurricane* was fiction. The issue was tense. Laura secretly convened with Athenian club members. They advised Laura to continue her writing, and let Rose find original stories.

Despite differences, a mother-daughter collaboration jelled. Rose's experience was essential in prepping *Little House* manuscripts. This was the process: Laura drafted each book. Rose typed and edited. Mother and daughter conferred, disagreed, and compromised. Rose preferred to focus on her writings, but viewed her mother's books as needed income. Agent George Bye negotiated contracts with Harper.

Children's publishing flourished in the 1930s, but Rose wanted no association with it. Laura's independence as an author was nurtured. Privately Laura credited Rose saying, "Part of the praise belongs to you." *Little House on the Prairie* was published in 1935, the same year Rose's *Old Home Town* appeared.

At the farmhouse Rose was surrogate mother to John and Al Turner, orphaned brothers. The boys attended Mansfield High. At home, she was supportive, watching over the boys' grades, athletics, health and friendships. A clubhouse was built; it soon became a high school hangout with parties, dancing, food and fun. While the boys were at school, Laura and Rose worked on *On the Banks of Plum Creek*.

Laura at the time of the Detroit trip. "I am 5'2" with white hair and blue eyes."

On the Banks of Plum Creek needed major revision. Rose insisted that Laura stick to a theme. She advised her mother to "stay inside Laura" for authentic characterization. During the book's writing Rose left the farm. She moved to Columbia, Missouri to research a new book. Work on "Plum Creek" continued via mail.

Rose's move to Columbia ended eight years on the farm. For awhile John and Al stayed on with a housekeeper, though Rose was finished with the place. She was sure war was inevitable so she sent John and Al to bum around Europe before it "blew up." In New York City Rose started a serial for *Saturday Evening Post*: a pioneer story titled "Free Land."

With Rocky Ridge farmhouse empty, Manly and Laura moved back to their beloved home. The Rock House was rented.

When *Plum Creek* was published in the fall of 1937 Laura went to the J.L. Hudson's Book Fair in Detroit. Harper's staff was thrilled to meet her, along with audiences of children, educators and librarians. Silas Seal of Mansfield drove the Wilders' new Chrysler to Detroit; Manly enjoyed the ride. While Laura spoke and signed books, the men toured Detroit. Manly savored The Henry Ford Museum, filled with artifacts he recalled.

The Detroit visit was Laura's only experience with major book promotion. She was then involved in writing *By the Shores of Silver Lake,* with more books planned to complete her series. Through correspondence the mother-daughter teamwork flourished, though Rose was swamped with work in New York. The "Free Land" serial was a huge success in early 1938; Rose's fee was enormous: $25,000. It barely squared her debts, but paid for a country house in Danbury, Connecticut, the first home she ever owned. In book form *Free Land* was a best seller.

Laura and Manly traveled to the west coast in May 1938. Silas Seal drove, and his wife Neta came along. The trip bonded the Wilders and Seals. The friendship enriched them all. They saw each other often when they were back in Mansfield.

Manly, Neta Seal and Laura in Yellowstone National Park.

By the Shores of Silver Lake was published in 1939, the same year that Manly and Laura made their final trip to South Dakota. *The Long Winter* was out in 1940, followed by *Little Town on the Prairie* in 1941. The finale was *These Happy Golden Years*, which completed the series in 1943.

The manuscript for "These Happy Golden Years".

Laura Ingalls Wilder's books were all published within eleven years; she was one of America's most distinguished children's writers. A book critic summed up the eight volume series with these words: *"No one can make the past come alive more vividly and sympathetically … Mrs. Wilder's art is difficult to analyze. It is made up of simplicity, honesty and the ability to tell a beautiful story."*

VII. Really Retired

America was deeply involved in World War II when Laura completed her books. She and Manly savored the peace of Rocky Ridge, but followed war news closely. Laura and Rose discussed politics and their dislike for FDR in correspondence. Manly, Laura and Rose were opposed to government aid to citizens, and federal programs which ignored work ethic and self-sufficiency.

After lifetimes of hardship and labor, Laura and Manly took pride in their achievements. They were really retired, and simply enjoyed Rocky Ridge life.

Rose stopped writing fiction, but did a political column called "Rose Lane Says." Her views were anti-New Deal. Big government threatened personal liberty, she wrote. Rose's appearances on radio were so extreme that people questioned her passion. She made national headlines, criticizing Social Security as dangerous fraud on the American people. Rose clashed with a Danbury police officer who investigated her and asked her to explain her views. Friends feared that Rose, always a firebrand, was becoming a political crackpot. The FBI maintained a file on her.

In 1943 Rose published *The Discovery of Freedom*. The book traced the struggle of humanity against repression and authority. Manly and Laura found the book fascinating. Rose's thesis matched their own passion for personal independence. Rose wrote: "No man's security is any greater than his own self-reliance." That summed up the Wilder family's lifestyle.

There were no more financial worries on Rocky Ridge. In the '40s, Laura's royalties reached $8,000-$10,000 annually. She and Manly groused over income taxes. Laura declared that was a factor in her decision to stop writing. Rose avoided income tax altogether, limiting her earnings to less than $1,000 per year. After years of helping her parents financially, Rose was on the receiving end; Laura shared book royalties with her.

Wednesday was the Wilders' day to shop in Mansfield. They became less visible in town during the war years; their gas ration of four gallons a week limited travel. Manly's poor hearing made him seem more distant than he was, and problems with his foot slowed him. For these reasons, they attended church less frequently, although the Methodists held a special dinner for the Wilder's 58th anniversary in 1943. One last time, around their birthdays, Laura opened the parlor for an evening party. She still hosted club meetings, but enjoyed being a participant rather than the moving force she once was.

The Wilders were not reclusive, but newer generations knew little of their earlier activity in Mansfield life. Laura decided "to get out when the getting was good" instead of helping with the Methodists' 35¢ chicken dinners. She did not want to be patiently endured by younger people.

"The goat by the tree gave 217 8/10 lbs. of milk in May," Almanzo wrote on this snapshot he sent to Rose.

Each morning, Manly tended to chores. The goats and Jack the donkey were the only barn residents. Manly doted on the goats, training them to ascend a platform at milking time. He claimed that grazing goats in poison ivy kept him immune from the plants. He shared goat milk with friends, and supplied it for babies with delicate digestions.

Manly planted the garden each spring, and maintained pastures by planting grasses. Wartime manpower shortage was a problem; it was difficult to hire anyone to help. "To care for a ten room farmhouse is no small job," Laura said, though it was easier now with her tank-style vacuum sweeper. The wood stove still served for cooking and heat, and Manly split the firewood. In a corner of the kitchen, like a banished child, stood a small electric range. Laura used it in summer, or, as if ashamed of her indulgence, to quickly boil water. She sewed, mended, and did fancy work. In the evenings she and Manly played cribbage, listened to the radio, and read magazines, newspapers and books.

Laura was constantly busy with the fame resulting from the *Little House* stories. Awards arrived, including a citation from the Pacific Northwest Library Association and the *New York Herald Tribune* Book Prize. Readers sent gifts of fruit, candy, books,

Mary and Jack discuss their favorite Wilder book at the Pomona, California Public Library. Mary's family called on Laura while driving through Missouri.

and handicrafts. The reader letters showed how deeply Laura's pioneer tales enriched lives. Children and adults asked questions about the book characters, requested autographs and pictures, and begged for more stories. Here are some of the comments she received:

"I can't tell you how much I like your books. I could read them a thousand times and still read them some more," wrote Joyce from New Hampshire.

Paul from Wisconsin wrote *"I like them so well that I bought the series for myself. I earned the money picking beans on hot August days."*

An Iowa teacher described her daily reading sessions: *"The children have really lived with you in Wisconsin, Indian Territory, New York, on Plum Creek, and in Dakota Territory. They call you Laura, just as if you were their nearest and dearest friend."*

A New York mother sent a sugar ration stamp, saying: *"Perhaps your sugar allotment is not sufficient to permit you to make Mr. Wilder gingerbread or a pie as often as you would like to."*

A girl named Greta wrote that her teacher read her class *These Happy Golden Years*, and said *"I'm always dreaming about you."*

A parent wished that *"I could put into words how much you and your family have become a part of our lives — your books are great books…because they have the simplicity and honesty of reality."*

A Chicago educator told of his sons' love for the books read aloud in their own vacation log cabin: *"I read 'Little House In The Big Woods' to them countless times. Truly, that story contributed to the dreams of our family to have our own log cabin on Whitefish Lake."*

Laura answered each of those letters — thousands of them. Sometimes the task overwhelmed her, but she always responded. She said she could not bear to disappoint a child. Harper & Brothers issued a publicity folder about the *Little House* books and the Wilders; that helped answer some of the questions and included several photos of Laura.

Here is one of Laura's typical replies, a 1945 letter to a California classroom:

Dear Children,

Please excuse my answering your letters all in one. I have so many letters that I write schools just one letter. I am glad you like my stories and thank you for inviting me to visit you.

Sister Carrie and I are the only ones of our family now living. I was two years younger than Mary; Carrie is three years younger than I am, and Grace was ten years younger than I. I am seventy eight.

Now there is a problem for you to figure out how old Carrie is. Mary never married. She got along fine in the College for the Blind, came home when she graduated and lived there happy and busy with her music, her books, and her work. She knitted, and made pretty things with beads and helped Ma with the housework and sewing.

Grace married and lived on her husband's farm a few miles from DeSmet. Carrie married a mine owner in the Black Hills, S. Dakota and went there to live. Neither Carrie nor Grace had any children.

It was more than seventy years ago when Almanzo owned Starlight and more than sixty years ago when he owned the Morgan horses. So they are all gone now, for horses do not live that long.

Almanzo and I live by ourselves on our farm, though we don't farm now. We are too old to do the farm work and cannot hire anyone. The farm is all is pasture, meadow and woods.

We used to keep a lot of stock but now we have only four milk goats and a burro. Burros are fun and ours is such a pet he is spoiled. We like to live here, but wish our only child did not live so far away. Her name is Rose Wilder Lane and her home is in Connecticut. Her adopted son is in the Coast Guard.

I never learned to care very much for Miss Wilder. She died long ago. No one calls me Flutterbudget now. No one but Pa ever did.

I thank you for all your nice letters and am

Sincerely your friend,
Laura Ingalls Wilder

Adults were interested in Laura's current life. To them, her responses were more personal, as in this 1944 letter:

"I have worn my hair short for a good many years, tailored cut in the back and long enough in front to curl and fluff around my face. No permanents, just a homemade curl. I never smoked nor drank nor do I wear any skirts as short as the fashion is. Do not paint my finger nails, nor use rouge, just keep my complexion good and powder lightly. By no stretch of the imagination could I ever have been called ultra-modern."

With Laura's address in *Who's Who*, readers knew where the Wilders were, and started to visit. A regular stream of cars arrived at the gate, hoping to meet Laura and Manly. Tongue-tied kids, teachers and librarians, grateful parents … all hoped for a few words with their favorite writer. Laura graciously dealt with the visitors.

In August, 1942 "The Scribblers" a Topeka writers' club, was invited to Rocky Ridge. Laura gave a tour of the house, pointing out where she and Rose wrote. When asked about her own favorite books, Laura laughed, saying: "People I wouldn't associate with I don't want to see in a book." After tea, the club departed "feeling privileged to have met this charming author and mother … certain that Mrs. Wilder, both in her books and out of her books, expressed the American Way of Life as no other author has."

Nearing the ages of 80 and 90, the future of their land concerned the Wilders. In 1943 they sold the Rock House and its surrounding forty acres to Harland and Gireda Shorter, an energetic young couple with two sons. The Shorters managed the local farmers' cooperative, and established a modern dairy and poultry operation on the Wilder land.

"Mr. and Mrs. Wilder were the kind of people you couldn't help but like. Mrs. Wilder was especially jolly," said Mrs. Shorter. On a

Sunday morning in 1948, the Shorters were invited to visit. Manly and Laura offered to sell them the rest of the farm for $8,000. The Shorters accepted, and agreed to give the Wilders a life estate on the house, barn and surrounding acres. Manly wanted a monthly payment of $50. "That way *I'll* have some money," he said.

The Wilders were pleased that good stewardship of their land was assured. Rose was not interested in the place, but shared in the proceeds of the sale; her parents never forgot her earlier contributions. She hadn't been home since 1936. Her life was rooted in Danbury. Mansfield was a closed chapter in her life.

Neta and Silas Seal became the Wilders' surrogate children. They spent Sundays together, shared meals, and took drives through the Ozarks and trips to Springfield. Silas drove, since Manly was denied insurance

At Pt. Lookout, Missouri, October 1944. Neta and Silas Seal, Laura and Carrie.

because of his age. When Carrie Ingalls Swanzey came to visit in 1944, they all toured *Shepherd of the Hills* country. It was Laura's last visit with Carrie, who died in 1946. This left Laura the last surviving member of her family.

Manly suggested moving to the Seals' apartment building in town. There were four apartments there (Neta and Silas occupied one of them), plus sleeping rooms. Manly liked socializing at the Seals' gas station next door. Farther down the street he could nab Pete Freeman from The Bank of Mansfield, for a game of pool. Laura wanted no part of town life. During Manly's attempt to persuade her, she reminded him that there would be no place for his tools in town. Her point was made; Manly said no more.

Late in 1946 Laura attended a Methodist-Presbyterian church ladies' meeting. She got a lot of attention, since her presence was rare at such events. She disliked leaving Manly alone, since he was not feeling well. Someone asked if they were going to Chicago for a celebration of Laura's birthday. No, Laura said, they weren't going because of Manly's health.

A new Mansfield resident met Laura at the meeting, Irene Lichty. She noted Laura's vivid presence: "She was a gentlewoman, as we might call a man a gentleman. She wasn't gregarious, but pleasant to everyone. She was petite and beautiful, a bit demure. She was well-dressed, looking like a Dresden doll. Her friends loved her dearly. I was fortunate to be among them, also my husband and my mother. She asked me if I read her books. 'They're children's books, aren't they?' I said casually. She looked at me, and said, ' You read them.'"

Irene and her husband Lewis knew Manly slightly; he seemed so reticent. Once, Irene saw him park his Chrysler at Aunt Daisy Freeman's; he was delivering goat milk. "How tiny he looks in that big car," she thought. "I knew Aunt Daisy was in Springfield, so I told him so," Irene remembered. "He looked at me and said, 'Oh?' That was all."

On April 12, 1945 President Franklin Roosevelt died; that night a tornado swept through the Ozarks. It left Rocky Ridge without power and phone, with fallen trees blocking the driveway. The house was damaged, including a blown out window. Another adventure with Manly, Laura thought. Kerosene lamps were used while they were marooned for two weeks, until fallen trees were removed.

Beyond the farm, radio and newspapers informed the Wilders of a changing world. Truman, a Missourian they didn't particularly like, succeeded FDR as president. Rose declared that Truman was a liar. Horrible stories emerged from Europe after the German surrender, almost too shocking to believe. The war claimed many boys the Wilders knew; some returned; others died in faraway places. With the advent of the Atomic age, Laura remarked pensively, "Here's hoping the atom bomb test tonight will do no harm more than expected."

Ben, the Wilder bulldog, 1947.

After the war, translations of Laura's books were published in Germany and Japan, through a State Department program to re-educate the defeated countries about American values. General Douglas Mac Arthur promoted the *Little House* books in Japan. More translations followed and fan mail was included foreign postmarks, especially from Japan.

In 1945 a network radio adaptation of *The Long Winter* was produced. Another radio broadcast was aired from Chicago in

February 1947, when Laura turned 80, and Manly turned 90. The Carson, Pirie & Scott Department Store held a large birthday party for Chicago children who voted for Laura in a favorite author poll. Her name led the list. Laura sent 200 autographs for the children, and they signed an oversized plaque which joined other honors on the shelves of the library at Rocky Ridge.

That same year, Ursula Nordstrom, the Harper editor who nearly deified Laura, realized that the baby boomer generation was poised to become *Little House* readers. She envisioned a new edition of the books, lavishly illustrated. Her choice as artist was Garth Williams, whose work appeared in the 1945 success *Stuart Little*. Ursula asked Garth for full color oil paintings; when this proved too costly, they settled on color jackets, with soft pencil pictures throughout the books.

Garth knew nothing of Laura's Midwest, so in November 1947 he made a trek to meet the Wilders. Ever afterward, he spoke fondly of the visit, first spying Laura gathering pecans as he arrived. She seemed vibrant, jovial, and youthful. They went inside to visit with Manly. "There I stood with the hero and heroine of the books," Garth said. "What could be more exciting!" He looked over family photos, asked about current sites of the books, and sought Laura's opinion about portraying her characters.

To Garth's amazement, Laura made no specifications about the illustrations. To her, the text was all-important. Armed with her

Laura and Manly at home, 1948.

directions, Garth headed off to research locales in Kansas, Minnesota, and South Dakota. Garth steeped himself in Americana for the job, but he drew a sizeable amount of the art in Italy.

News from Detroit in December, 1948 surprised the Wilders. The Detroit Public Library announced that a new branch would be named for Laura Ingalls Wilder, the first such honor for a living person and for a woman. Laura's name joined Edison, Franklin, and Jefferson as library namesakes. The Wilders were invited to the dedication in May. "Mr. Wilder's general health is better but he is ninety two years old and not strong. It is not safe for him to be alone … and I cannot leave home," Laura explained.

Laura wrote a message for the event, and donated two of her penciled manuscripts, two of her school books and other memorabilia to the Detroit Library.

Though feeble, Manly planted the garden that spring. In July he suffered a heart attack. Laura tended him at home, leaving him with a friend only long enough to make necessary trips to town. Neta Seal often slipped in late at night, sleeping on the porch, so the Wilders would not be alone. Slowly, Manly recovered.

The Wilders were alone on Sunday morning, October 23, when Manly slipped away. Laura summoned the Seals, and they found her clinging to Manly, not wanting to believe he was gone. Sixty four years together, filled with deep love and companionship, were now over.

VIII. MANSFIELD'S MRS. WILDER

Rose arrived for Manly's funeral, and stayed on for a week. Whatever was said between mother and daughter is unknown. Surely Rose invited Laura to stay with her in Danbury. A friend spent a few nights, until Laura sent her home. She did not want a live-in companion, but she was exhausted from the strain of nursing Manly, and her thoughts were jumbled from shock.

A friend said that "… for Mrs. Wilder, all was well with the world until Manly died." She was stoic, though "… so lonely for Almanzo".

Laura decided to stay on Rocky Ridge, feeling secure with the Elmore family across the road and the Joneses in a new house to the east. The Seals spent Sunday afternoons with her, and invited her to dinner, as did others. Laura no longer cooked company dinners, but entertained friends at Frederick's, her favorite restaurant in Cabool.

Neta phoned her morning and evening, and drove her on errands. Laura called the town taxi if needed. Groceries were delivered to her. She ordered healthy foods. In winter deliveries included boxes of citrus fruits, and specially ordered kumquats.

Laura resumed church-going, riding along with the Joneses. She liked visiting after church, but once was overcome with emotion and hurried away. She wrote a note to friends, explaining that the closing hymn had also been used at Manly's

Summer, 1950. Highway 60 curves into Mansfield (in the background).

funeral. "I could barely speak to anyone," she said.

The two young Jones boys, Roscoe and Sheldon, became Laura's joy. They stopped daily, bringing her mail, doing chores, cutting grass, and helping with heavy cleaning. The boys found her a smiling, loving, grandmotherly figure. She told them pioneer stories, and was pleased that their family read her books aloud in the evenings, just as countless others did across America.

To the brothers she confided feelings shared with no one else. Checks and business related to her books was a nuisance, she grumbled. "I have more money than any one person has a right to," she said. The boys helped sort fan mail and when boxes of candy arrived as gifts they helped eat it.

When Roscoe and Sheldon were in school, Mrs. Jones walked over with gifts of bread and cookies. "Mrs. Wilder was always smiley, full of witty sayings, quotes, and poetry," she recalled. "I was there on my 40th birthday, and mentioned that 'life begins at 40.'

Eyes twinkling, she replied: "No dear, 'life begins at 80!'"

Others phoned and visited. The Lichtys included Laura on drives and restaurant dinners. One Mother's Day she surprised them by ordering whale meat. Irene was always thoughtful and solicitous, and how Laura enjoyed joshing and kidding with Lewis. Propriety was more relaxed, and she could freely visit and joke with men she knew. She and Mr. Craig had a running bet that they would live to 100. On her Wednesday town visits, she stopped at the *Mansfield Mirror* to discuss politics and current affairs with the editor Ralph Watters. They became very close, and she was a trusted counselor when his unhappy marriage ended.

Laura dining at Fredrick's Cafe in Cabool, Missouri, 1954

With Manly gone, Laura had time to be "a celebrated author." She spoke at a story hour at the Springfield library, and addressed a college class. The Athenians held "Laura Ingalls Wilder Day" for her in Hartville. Mansfield fourth graders came to Rocky Ridge to see the house, eat gingerbread, and visit with Laura. Later, Laura visited classes at the school, where the children greeted her with the jingle: *"Good morning Mrs. Wilder, how are you?"*

Laura saw many changes in 1950s Mansfield. A shoe factory, drive-in theater, golf course, and a "Butter Day" celebration were established. A hospital opened, and Laura was a patient there. A motel was built on part of Rocky Ridge, though out of Laura's view. TV antennas were everywhere, but Laura disliked television. She mentioned seeing a flying saucer sail over the farm one day.

Laura's idea of progress was the new library in town. For years The Athenians worked for a county library system. When established, the Mansfield branch was in a private home, then in the Bay Shoe Store, and finally in rented quarters. Laura went there each week to borrow books. She was especially keen on western paperbacks by Luke Short and Zane Grey.

Docia Holland, the county librarian, became her close friend. Laura loved going with Docia on the library's bookmobile runs. Up and down the hills the bookmobile swooped, bringing reading to remote parts of Wright County. In St. Louis another bookmobile made its rounds ... one named for Laura Ingalls Wilder.

In 1951 the library sponsored a national card shower for Laura's 84th birthday. Nearly a thousand greetings resulted. Then plans were made to name the library for Laura Ingalls Wilder on September 28, 1951.

Amid high school band music, a huge floral display from the Craigs, speeches, presentation of a display case, and crowds of area people, the Wilder Library was named. Laura was particularly radiant that day. Wearing her wine velvet dress, she spoke feelingly, saying "I cannot tell you how much I

At the naming of the Wilder Library in Mansfield.

41

value your friendship and the honor you have done me … From my heart I thank you!"

The library showcase featured Wilder books and mementoes. Laura brought in Manly's cane collection, and the trowel used in building each house from Malone to Mansfield. She added for display the sickle used by Manly and his father. The library filled a need for pilgrimage when visitors could not meet Laura herself.

Laura once remarked that she thought Mansfield had forgotten her. After the library dedication she knew better. The motto that day was from Voltaire: *"By appreciation we make excellence in others our own property."*

No one could have said it better.

"…HAVING WRIT, MOVES ON"

Rose made regular trips to Rocky Ridge during the 1950s. The summer after Manly's death, her Danbury friends, the Morgans, drove her to Mansfield. While the women visited, Al Morgan made needed repairs to the farmhouse. In 1953 Rose and her friends visited again. They wanted Laura to join them on a winter trip to Florida, but her age interfered with "the ability and desire to wander far."

Rose at Rocky Ridge during her 1950 visit.

Rose's solo trips were made by plane to Springfield; Laura sent a driver to meet her. Rose slipped quietly in and out of town, though Laura insisted that she present herself at the newspaper office so her visit would be mentioned in the paper. *The Mansfield Mirror* was important to Laura. She read it aloud to Rose, commenting with pleasure over those mentioned. Rose was more cynical, railing against provincialism and lack of intellectual stimulation in her hometown. She resented lingering clannishness in Mansfield. "We only came in 1894, and are still 'furriners'," she fumed.

Evidence suggests that Laura made a short trip to Danbury, accompanying Rose on her return flight. Laura traveling by airplane … an amazing thought. Of such progress Laura said, "There are some modern things that are much better than in pioneer times, but if I had my choice I would much rather live in the old days as I did than now with all the modern conveniences." Rose said her mother stood with feet firmly planted in the 19th century. Laura dropped the Democratic party and voted Republican for Eisenhower in the 1950s.

Though her books and beliefs bound Laura to the past, she was curious about the future. When Aunt Daisy Freeman confided that she was ready to die, Laura pushed the thought away, replying, "Oh no! I want to stay around to see what happens!"

In 1953 the newly illustrated edition of the *Little House* books was published with great acclaim. Reviewers were lavish in praise, advertising was widespread, and sales soared. Laura complimented the updated books, but secretly preferred the first edition art. Laura understood marketing, and cooperated with any requests that her publishers made. Harper produced a film called *Mrs. Wilder and Her Books* for added promotion.

Along with a deluge of gifts and cards for her 87th birthday, Laura received announcement of a major award bearing her name. For years librarians were dismayed that Laura never received the Newbery Medal, perhaps because her books were a series. So the Children's Library Association created the *Laura Ingalls Wilder Award*. Laura received the first medal. Unable to travel to the June 1954 American Library Association meeting, Laura sent along an appreciative letter to be read.

Laura felt guilty that Neta Seal spent so much time driving her on errands. In the winter of 1954 she sent Jim Hartley, the town

The new Oldsmobile

taxi-man, to buy her a car. He came back with an expensive green air conditioned Oldsmobile. Jim kept the car in town, on call when Laura needed transportation. The arrangement was secret. Laura was anxious to avoid "talk". When a friend referred to her new car, Laura asked how she knew

it was hers. The response: "Why, everyone in town knows it's your car!" Laura sat at her kitchen table, shaking with amused laughter. There were few secrets in a small town.

Jim Hartley, a widower, was much younger than Laura. He became

"Children's Book Week at Brown's Book Store in Springfield was a great success. It was Saturday, November 15 (1952). I autographed 200 books ..."
— Laura Ingalls Wilder

a good friend. He drove her to church, where young boys ogled the car. Laura and Jim went for drives through the countryside, stopping at local restaurants. Jim's sudden death devastated Laura. Virginia, his daughter-in-law, comforted Laura, assuring her she would take over as driver.

Laura sailed into her eighties, amazingly spry. Her doctor pronounced her physically much younger than her years, despite arthritis and eye problems. She had bouts of "nerves", a heart attack, and even mumps. Her blood pressure sometimes soared, but she was usually robust. Her real problem was undiagnosed diabetes. This was a family curse; both Carrie and Grace died from it, and possibly Ma and Mary.

Through each illness, Neta Seal was faithful. Neta nursed Laura through a fall which required stitches in her forehead. Laura phoned Rose, making light of the mishap. Rose appreciated Neta's loyalty. But she knew her mother was as independently tough as she was. "We are both almost indestructible," Rose said.

Despite her resilience, Laura prepared for the future. She wrote a will, leaving her considerable savings and royalties to Rose. Upon Rose's death the royalties were to divert to the Laura Ingalls Wilder Library. Earlier, Laura offered to build a permanent library on the square, but local inaction interfered. She remembered her friends;

Laura bequeathed her household goods to the Seals. To others she gave keepsakes, jewelry, dishes, and the family Bible.

Laura was philosophical about life and death. For years she enjoyed *The Rubaiyat of Omar Khayyam*, and often quoted one of her favorite lines: *"The moving finger writes, and having writ, moves on."* She repeated "A Prayer for Those in Advanced Age" and wrote "Even so, my life facing the future sees no end."

Laura's Bible always sat next to her favorite rocking chair, with her list of favorite scripture references. One winter she memorized the Book of John. She spoke little of her personal religious beliefs, but appreciated friends' prayers. "One needs the prayers of friends," she said. Another of her favored quotes was *"He prayeth best who loveth best/All things great and small/For the dear God who loveth us/He made and loveth all."*

March 1953: The Failings' visit to Rocky Ridge made Laura nostalgic.

Until 1955 Laura answered her reader mail, and then Harpers took over. When well, Laura continued to see visitors who arrived, though she objected to those coming to stare at a celebrity. When ill, she did not answer the door. And it was not pleasant to have surprise company with her hair in curlers, or early in the morning. When Rose was visiting she offered to make "short shrift" of an arriving car. "No, Rose they came a long way to see me" Laura responded. She stepped out to meet her callers.

Laura savored visitors from her past. Elmer and Berta Hader, the author-illustrator team stopped. Many DeSmet area people

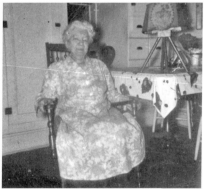

Laura wanted to change her housecoat for Dr. Failing's photos. "Don't worry," he said. "Your dress will look like silk in this picture."

stopped by to see her. When Dr. and Mrs. Failing introduced themselves, Laura burst into tears, realizing that Hazel Failing was the daughter of her girlhood friend Dave Gilbert. She wanted them to stay on with her. She beamed for the doctor's camera, as she sat in her rocking chair. Another surprise was her Cousin Lena's granddaughter's call. Many, many educators and librarians made the trek to Rocky Ridge.

In 1955, Laura was invited to DeSmet's 75th anniversary celebration. Aubrey Sherwood, editor of *The DeSmet News,* wrote her about the event, which included a local talent play of *"The Long Winter"*, adapted from Hallmark's radio script. There was talk in town of a memorial to the Ingalls family. Laura said she would love to re-visit DeSmet, but her traveling days were over. These were times for quiet days at home. Laura filled the time playing solitaire, making a scrapbook of her career and personal clippings, and piecing a quilt.

Her books still provided pleasant surprises. In the fall of 1955 Laura watched a St. Louis television broadcast about the *Little House* books. She also gave permission for her agent to explore the possibility of a *Little House* television series.

Ruth Gagliardo, "The Book Lady" of Kansas, librarian and children's reading advocate, visited Laura at Rocky Ridge.

Just before Thanksgiving 1956, Rose arrived and found Laura in a diabetic crisis. By ambulance they went to the Springfield hospital, where diagnosis and correct treatment restored Laura. Rose, who just turned 70, spent the December days in her mother's hospital room. Even there, hospital staff asked for autographs. Laura thought

Rose was teasing when she read her an article in the Springfield newspaper about her illness. She was very pleased that people were concerned. And then a long scroll bearing good wishes of hundreds of Springfield children was delivered to her room.

After Christmas Laura returned to Rocky Ridge. Rose had the rooms freshly painted and wallpapered, and Laura happily showed visitors the improvements. She was flustered, however, when dial phones reached Mansfield. She now had a phone number. It was: WA 4-3777. Progress … no longer did an operator connect calls.

Rose invited Laura to come to Danbury, but it was not her wish. So Rose remained on Rocky Ridge, with help from Virginia Hartley and others, caring for Laura. Cards and presents arrived for Laura's birthday, but she was slipping away. She died February 10, 1957, three days after her 90th birthday.

Laura was gone, but the legacy of her *Little House* books and her simple homespun philosophy continues to flourish. Laura Ingalls Wilder, pioneer and author, remains one of the world's best beloved authors.

THE DOOR IS OPEN AT ROCKY RIDGE FARM

A reader who visited Laura at Rocky Ridge wrote, "I wish arrangements could be made for her home to be kept as it is after she is gone, for the children who love her books." It was a wish others shared, in Mansfield and beyond.

Laura was aware that people envisioned her home as a memorial. Irene Lichty was the first to mention it directly. Laura listened quietly, saying only, "I've let my home get quite shabby...." Later Laura told Rose how pleased she was with the idea.

Within days after Laura's death a group of Mansfield citizens called on Rose, expressing a desire to keep the house on Rocky Ridge and its contents intact for readers to see. Rose, though grief-stricken, was agreeable, promising to help. As she examined her parents' keepsakes, she was amazed at the quantity of Americana in the family home. She labeled many items, and put them in safe-keeping until the museum transpired.

A charter was obtained for the Laura Ingalls Wilder Home Association. The first open house brought 500 visitors in May, 1957. Founder Memberships of $100 were sold to create a treasury. The Shorters offered to return the house and three acres of land to the Association at their cost. Rose contributed the purchase price. Regular tours commenced during summer months. Many Mansfield residents donated services and funds to the project.

Until her death in 1968 Rose was a behind-the-scenes force in the memorial's progress. In 1963 she donated funds to build a curators' home nearby. Lewis and Irene Lichty were named the first curators. In 1971, a museum building was constructed, with assistance from Roger Mac Bride.

The preservation of Rocky Ridge Farm has attracted visitors from all over the world. Over the years most of the original farmland has been purchased and secured, including the 1928 Rock House. The happy home the Wilders built is now one of America's great landmarks. The door is still open to visitors at Rocky Ridge Farm.